P9-DGQ-192

the field

the field

n
e
w
RIVERS
PRESS
MSUM

poems by
tim nolan

©2016 by Tim Nolan
First Edition
Library of Congress Control Number: 2015953388
ISBN: 978-0-89823-355-1

Cover and Interior Design by Jin Thieschafer
Author photo by Kate Nolan

The publication of *The Field* is made possible by the generous support
of Minnesota State University Moorhead, The McKnight Foundation, the
Dawson Family Endowment, and other contributors to New Rivers Press.

 THE McKNIGHT FOUNDATION

For copyright permission, please contact Frederick T. Courtright at
570-839-7477 or permdude@eclipse.net.

New Rivers Press is a nonprofit literary press associated with
Minnesota State University Moorhead.

Alan Davis, Director and Senior Editor
Nayt Rundquist, Managing Editor
Kevin Carollo, MVP Poetry Coordinator
Bayard Godsave, MVP Prose Coordinator
Thom Tammaro, Poetry Editor
Thomas Anstadt, Co-Art Director
Trista Conzemius, Co-Art Director
Wayne Gudmundson, Consultant
Suzanne Kelley, Consultant

Publishing Interns:
Laura Grimm, Anna Landsverk, Desiree Miller, Mikaila Norman

The Field Book Team:
Desiree Miller, Mikaila Norman

 Printed in the USA on acid-free, archival-grade paper.

The Field is distributed nationally by Small Press Distribution.

 New Rivers Press
c/o MSUM
1104 7th Avenue South
Moorhead, MN 56563
www.newriverspress.com

For Kate

Contents

I.

1 ...... Blank Page
2 ...... Black Fly
3 ...... Stray Words
4 ...... Self-Portrait as a Patch of Dirt
5 ...... Resume
7 ...... The Basement
9 ...... Heart
11 ...... Some Thoughts Came to Mind
12 ...... Barely
13 ...... Self-Portrait as a Busy Person
14 ...... Seasoned
16 ...... Failure
17 ...... Angle of Entry
18 ...... 12 Years Old

II.

21 ...... Roasted Chicken
22 ...... Catwork
23 ...... A Woman
24 ...... Self-Portrait as a Dog
25 ...... Shoes
27 ...... Pictures from a Funeral and a Graduation Party
29 ...... Sky in Spring
30 ...... Wind in Spring
31 ...... The Shoes of Teenage Boys
32 ...... What Comes Back
33 ...... Winter Sun at Dusk
34 ...... Whistling
35 ...... Our Midwestern Sky

III.

39 ...... Mother's Day
40 ...... Confusion
43 ...... Broken Hip

45 ...... Heavy
47 ...... Yes
49 ...... She
50 ...... Comfortable
51 ...... My Dead
52 ...... The Blue Light
53 ...... Yesterday

IV.

57 ...... Gettysburg
58 ...... Ice House
59 ...... A Vision
62 ...... Children of Myanmar Who Behave
           Like Japanese Soldiers
63 ...... Wood Smoke
64 ...... Windows On The World
65 ...... Museum
67 ...... Copley Square Hotel
68 ...... Devotions
70 ...... Café
71 ...... Cathedral
73 ...... Cemetery
74 ...... Red Wing Correctional Facility
76 ...... Leaving
77 ...... Song
79 ...... The Flow
80 ...... Talking
82 ...... Edgar Mitchell Coming Home
83 ...... Treasure
84 ...... The Field

Acknowledgments
About the Author
About New Rivers Press

Beyond myself, somewhere,
I wait for my arrival.

—Octavio Paz

Blank Page

All I have to do is jump
in like a swimmer
in my own lane.

Really it's more like
ironing a king-sized
sheet on a footstool.

Or looking for the "X"
that shows where I am
at the Mall of America.

Since I've said this much,
it's as if I have a lamp,
a table and a chair,

a little hooked rug,
a wife and children,
flowers in the windows.

Can you smell the shallots
sautéeing in the bubbling butter?
The first step in the best

recipe ever. (Now I'm just
making things up). You may
get tired of this. I could

start over. But you are still
hungry and I am still talking
and *this* might go on and on.

Black Fly

I'm keeping a pet fly
in the bathroom.

This morning as I took
a shower, he slept

upside down on the
molding around the door.

And as I dried off,
he came awake, buzzed

around the room,
landed on my arm,

as if to say "Good
morning."

The coincidence
of our bodies here

in a small, white-tiled
room with a mirror.

I do love him—as he flies
around my glowing face—

Stray Words

All the words are strays,
all of them are mutts.

From any number of them,
I chose these.

So they belong to me,
like my old dogs,

picked for their sweet
eyes from the pound.

They've been all around
the city—smelling garbage

and urine—they have a map
of the city in their noses.

Yet they always come back to me—
Scruffled—still loving me.

Self-Portrait as a Patch of Dirt

I've worn down the grass
in the front yard where I sit
in a green chair waiting
for something to happen

This patch of dry earth suits me
it looks as if I've shuffled my feet
in place to make this patch
of dry and dusty dirt

It's July so the Sun beats down
anyone can see I've been here
sitting in place
going nowhere at great speed

Resume

There was the era when Mario
was my waiter—in that coffee shop
on Astor Place—and the decade

of the movies of Billy Wilder—
I couldn't get enough of him—
Not to mention—the string

of inconsequential jobs involving
carrying boxes, envelopes,
books, magazine clippings from

this cabinet, file, in-box—
to that—Now that I think of it—
there should be a separate section

on the letters I wrote that enclosed
a notice, a subpoena, a little time bomb,
a threat, a caress, a regret—

With respect to the gaps
in the chronology—I was away,
incapacitated, on leave,

thinking about what I would do
next—how I would complete
the page, the chapter, complete

the line—I recall leaving
a voicemail, a note, a Post-It—
on your door, window, screen—

My intentions were to learn
Latin, Russian, Chinese, French
so I could be a diplomat,

photographer, filmmaker, potter—
but not a fireman, policeman,
gynecologist, economist—(I probably

should not include what I did not
mean to do)—All this before
I've even arrived at the list

of publications, conferences attended,
casual remarks I made
to someone I never saw again

And those special talents—I should
put that in bold, underlined
the ability to sleep with some sense

of purpose—the way I can widen
the space between my eyes
and my eyebrows without

appearing demented—my voice—
how I can lower it—making you
think you're losing your hearing—

A photographic memory?—only if
the photograph is blurred—coffee-stained—
frayed—*disappearing*—

The Basement

The basement in the old family house
contains a steam locomotive—
a Milwaukee Road 261 Engine.

We didn't wonder how it got there
since there was also a semi-rig
carrying six brand new Ford Fairlanes

each a different color not to mention
thousands of Gerber baby food jars
full of nuts and bolts and various

useless pieces of metal come from somewhere
also every edition of *Time* and *Life* saved
for the reason that—it's always good

to save *Time* and *Life*—and somehow
everyone was there even the dead
who had worked to collect these things—

the tin bands from the Folger coffee cans
wrapped tight on those metal rings—
and keys—a huge keychain of keys—

for doors in buildings torn down—
the doors locked—the leather
football helmet—the coconut made into

a dispenser of string—we all worked
very hard to clean up the basement
moving in all directions at once.

Did you notice how the old root cellar
became the inside of Notre Dame
once you turned that latch and walked in?

What other family would have a great
stained-glassed window in the shape
of a rose—the family symbol? Somebody

asked: "Whose tuba is this?" It was like
a party a reunion a wedding reception
where we played each part—the bride

the groom the drunk uncle the ring-bearer
and flower girl—all at once this well-lit
joy—we were all together to clean out

the basement—how could this be so much
fun?—someone asked: "How did Grandpa
get the 261 in the basement?"

Which now seems like a good question
even as the answer is obvious—
He drove in last night from Aberdeen.

Heart

As they monitor me

I say—*Heart*—dear one

Dear pump—dear flow
of me

I say—keep me dear heart

I say—you look like
liver and onions

Turns out
you are a Valentine

I know I've been
rough on you

I know all these years—
But you still

Do that regular thing
which I feel in my

Chest and in my arms
the pulse of you

Which is not me
and is me

And is not me—
and so—*Dear*

Heart—when you fail
I will think

So fondly of you—dear
beating—dear heart

I can feel you now

Some Thoughts Came to Mind

When I woke up this morning
I thought *I'm fucked*
which is often my thought

early in the morning—fucked
in every which way—don't need
to tell you why

just *I'm fucked* every which
way but Sunday—trust me—
I'm really fucked

But this only gets me so far
gets me to the point
where I can say *I'm not so fucked*

or *I'm only a little bit
fucked* if I don't
consider this or that

by the time I'm on
my way to work—somehow—
I'm not fucked at all

Barely

I barely made it across the lake—
Lake Harriet—I was twelve—
one mile swimming across
with *Donn Anderson*
(two "n's" in "Donn").

I barely made it back from
Somerset, Wisconsin—I was
barely sixteen—I met a great-great
cousin twice removed at the VFW—
an old man named *Paquin*.

Barely, I made it out of Calgary,
Alberta with a scar on my back—
an ache inside me
a sadness
I thought I could master.

I barely made it off that subway car—
the A train—only me and two
gang kids sizing me up. At the stop
for the Museum of Natural History
their menace suddenly vaporized.

I only just passed—I almost didn't
make the plane—I barely
made it to the end of the month—
I had enough.
I barely had enough.

I barely made the turn—
I made it home barely—we missed—
we barely missed each other—
like that bus-sized asteroid
barely missing the Earth.

Self-Portrait as a Busy Person

Here's a masquerade: when someone
proudly tells me how busy they are
I think they are flirting with death.

When I am busy I might as well be
in a rushing river. Once in a while
my head pops up. Mostly I'm underwater.

I cannot place myself as a busy person.
My natural inclination is to clear
the calendar and go

to a disaster movie or spend
the afternoon in a dark corner
nursing my freedom.

I don't want to be a busy person.
That's for someone else. The plate spinner
on *The Ed Sullivan Show*. He was a busy one.

Seasoned

Not just in the sense
of salt and pepper
but also sweat on the pillow
The smell of me
in the tweed sport coat
That combination of old
smoke and faded sunlight
Seasoned as the woodpile
the wood collapsing in on itself
the logs drying out
cell by cell becoming
light as paper crumbly
as a story I once knew
Seasoned by the seasons
The quiet nothing of snow
The urgent return of the bud
The long lazy lapping of the lake
The turning again toward
nothing seasoned as my old shoes
jumbled up in the closet
Everywhere I've walked
in panic and fear sometimes
shuffling along I'm hard on shoes
I wear them out in no time
making a hole like a bullet hole
in the leather sole seasoned
by weeds the burnt grass
the kids going off
so we finally take a breath

My nicotine-seasoned fingernails
something like the taste
of basalmic vinegar drizzled
on a green tomato
The wind the new kind of wind
I notice again as if for the first time
One season turning toward the next
with everything about to happen

Failure

He's been so close to me
that he's like a brother,
the younger brother I never had,

who was such a monumental
fuck-up that he was endearing,
despite the late-night calls,

the women calling late at night
looking for *Failure* just as he's
left the country, gone gray.

The women were desperate for *Failure*,
in a way they'd never be desperate
for me. *Don't you know his number?*

What number might that be?
When we were boys, we talked
late into the night—I'd like to say

the crystal radio was on, the one
we made together from a kit,
but that's just plain sentimental.

He said *You saved my life.*
I don't remember anything so dramatic.
He tried to be close.

Last I heard he was living with our sister,
Trouble, she's a whole other story,
with their two mean old dogs.

Angle of Entry

Long ago on TV
they said if the astronauts

in their tin-foil capsule
didn't make the proper

angle of entry
they would burn up.

That landed on me—
I felt I was falling

and needed to pay attention
to the edges rushing past.

To not stray too far
from the central corridor

of my falling.
I learned that much from TV.

12 Years Old

If I had five bucks
in my pocket

I would go
downtown for lunch.

Still doing it.
Many lunches.

Reading a book.
Or this scribbling.

I'm so happy—
to be the same one.

*Who shall say I am not
the happy genius of my household?*

—William Carlos Williams

Roasted Chicken

I'm writing this on the cutting board after
one hour of the Amish chicken roasting in the oven.

How can I say this other than directly?—
He is beautiful—brown and still cooking here

On the cutting board—*he's so beautiful*—all fat
in the breast—his legs sticking out—I salted him

All over—upside and down—in the dark cavity
of him—the salt draws in the moisture of him.

Praise to his little absent brain—his beak—his
pecking intentions for the bit of grain—I'm sorry

But hungry—writing here in red ink—the splotched
grease of him—smeared here with my words—

Catwork

The old cat keeps peeing
around the house

Various places for peeing
the back door the bottom

Of the stairs right in front
of the refrigerator

The old cat manages to place
himself always in my path

He anticipates my path
and settles there

Right where my bare foot falls
on him and he cries out

Like a squeeze toy runs away
to exactly the next place I'll be

He already knows where I'll be
like *clockwork* or *catwork* to know

In one's essence what will happen
that's why he waits for the Sun

On the arm of the green chair
gazing East in his own good time

A Woman

With a big butt
and two tiny dogs
walks by. She

calls one of the dogs
Buddy. She says
Come on Buddy.

Then a guy with
a big butt runs by.
He isn't really

running *he is so slow*
listening to music
I cannot hear.

Now it's just me
for awhile,
that's fine.

And it's quiet
except for the yippy
dog around the corner.

He's been outside
long enough
he says in yips—

I want to come in—
which I understand
completely.

Self-Portrait as a Dog

I would be a golden retriever
eager but a little dumb.

I would jump in your lap if
I wasn't so big. But my eyes,

they would melt you and my
profound snout would cause you

to think of the helmeted Greeks.
Those years of battle at Troy.

I would bring back something
for you, a slobbery rock from

the battlements at Troy. You would
treasure my gift. I want you

to throw my rock across the lawn
so it will land in a great earthly thud.

I love that sound.

Shoes

They are having a shoe sale.
70% off. I want to get shoes

For everyone in the family—
boots, slippers, loafers—

I come to understand the difference
between men's sizes and women's.

I am obsessed with fitting
everyone—based upon my sense of them—

Which might not be their sense—
So, I send pictures to them

Across the country—of shoes—
shoes posed in a certain light

To show the wonderful stitching
or the solid tread

I entice them with shoes
I can't get my wife to say "Yes,"

To shoes that could belong
to a mailman or a nun

"But they're 70% off," I say,
and she wisely notes—*If worth*

Nothing to me—70% off—
is nothing. I know. I learned

That much of math in school.
But it seems too good to be true.

That's almost nothing
for shoes that used to cost

Something. I can tell you—
as I look down at my brown

Heritage Chukkas No. 9017—that I
am very happy with these shoes.

And I want you to be too.
So I buy boxes of shoes and ship

Them off. I want to be with
each of you as you walk down

Madison Avenue or Boylston Street
or in the hills above a little river town—

You might think—*No matter what
I have these shoes*—Which

In some other time would be
the greatest possible blessing.

See my shoes? Standing in the corner.
Ready to walk away. They fit just right.

Pictures from a Funeral and
a Graduation Party

Here he is in his Army uniform
looking young and determined.

There she is—wearing a *101 Dalmatians* costume
for Halloween.

He's beside her in a striped polo shirt.
All of this was years ago.

Here he is at his first communion staring
into the face of God.

He looks like one of the *Little Rascals*.
His hair is plastered down.

While she is an infant in a laundry basket
looking up at her mother.

The pictures are on display boards
at both places.

I am confused about where I am.

He is sitting on a dock up North—beside
his son who is beside his grandson.

The fish are not biting.

And she is surrounded by books—flopped down on her bed—she has fallen asleep.

Here he is a few weeks ago—at another graduation party. He smiles.

He seems to be looking past the camera to someplace else.

She is taking this picture of him.

Sky in Spring

The funny bungalows across the street
with pastel trims

the Winter trees all gray and stark
and the rangy bushes by the house

the new paint on the sides of the house
the yellow light above the door

the *No Soliciting* sign Frank bought
feeling a need to protect us

the gray sky up above the endless stream
of airplanes coming in and going out

the sad men and women in their cheap suits
their tired luggage their dangling name tags

trying to escape some future humiliation
What have I ever learned?

Except waiting which I only do well in this spot
of my own devising *I'm going nowhere*

within my high forehead anything
might happen

Wind in Spring

Blowing me around blowing
my papers and my eyelashes

blowing the ash off my cigarette
onto my brown sweater

blowing the fresh topsoil against the house
blowing the box kite with its delicate

tissue panels and balsa frame
blowing and tugging the kite string

I've held myself against all winds
the sharp Winter wind from Winnipeg

the small breeze in the corner of my brain
the rain and wind and hail

bouncing off the roof of the orange car
in the South Dakota storm

Now I realize
the wind has always loved me

The Shoes of Teenage Boys

At the front door the shoes are
amazing combinations of some

plastic and some unknown
material developed by NASA.

Even at rest the shoes have
the urgency of teenage boys

the jumping, etc., as a
courtship display. Now they rest

at the front door in skewed
and knock-kneed and pigeon-toed

repose *they mostly are very large*
the shoes—at rest but not for long.

The shoes are designed to appeal
as faces so the teenage boys

looking down into their faces
can go out into the wide world.

What Comes Back

You set the plate
down on the table and laugh

at my small joke—
we are on to each other—

not that we know everything—
something comes back

in the Midwestern equivalent
of the ebb tide—with the wind

over the tall grass—
the bushes around our house growing

wild and rangy until we cut them back
and the dried putty cracking

in the windows until I angle in fresh
putty that smells of linseed oil

We sleep in tangled
limbs—our heads turned—

our mouths open—if you listen closely
we are singing

Winter Sun at Dusk

Smeared orange
and smoky lavender

the steady cars steaming
through the cold

the white parcels of snow
on the flat roofs downtown

the lights coming on
in the empty offices

the old pictures of my kids
on the window ledge

the wide and lascivious Sun
setting through the cold

my face in the darkening window
the orange and red and fire out there

Whistling

He wanted to be a bird
whistling
making it up.

We could hear him
whistling
down the sidewalk.

His song was always
complicated
but finally joyful.

He didn't need
any words
to sing.

Just whistles
and trills
and elegant loops.

He wanted to be a bird.
Turns out
that's what happened.

Our Midwestern Sky

We know we are nowhere
but because we are here
we look up

All the clouds go east
except tonight the clouds
float west in a strange current

Like ships that should head
toward home but instead
float out in a low wind

Toward the far reaches
we are the far reaches
we've always known this

And I said, let grief be a fallen leaf
at the dawning of the day.

—Patrick Kavanagh

Mother's Day

Driving around Lake Harriet
with my Mom

We're listening
to Beethoven or someone

And she is directing
the orchestra and all

Of us really—she has always
wanted to be in charge

Because she's very good at it—
and then she notices—

My pudgy fingers—and she's right—
and then—I'm her little baby boy—

Confusion

I.

I could tell you how she tried to brush her teeth
with the arthritis lotion or smeared her face

with toothpaste thinking it was skin lotion
or saw the mouse running across her feet and caught

her breath like a little girl. There was no mouse
there was no cat to catch no mouse that was the problem.

I could tell you how she checked to make sure
she was not one of the dead that she was on this side

still on our team. I told her she was.
I could tell you how she remains sweet but frightened

you would say *What a nice old lady* (in her
rocking chair) (she doesn't have a rocking chair).

Here's the problem—the mice wake her always *always*
in the middle of the night. She can't ever sleep.

II.

She was confused she is
confused she talks a lot

but each word leads into
a cul-de-sac turning around

outside a big storm black
sky downpours of rain

which she doesn't notice
some things go on and on

i.e., the weather the Sun &
the Moon she is in a swirling

eddy a backwater
of a great river circling

around she sits on the edge
of her bed her eyes

wide with wonder she seems
so little her pupils wide open

III.

Yesterday she was focused on dogs
all the dogs of her life—*Pat, Sean, Kip,*

Nikki, Bridie—all somehow Irish
dogs. She was interested in the colors

of all these dogs—their many varieties
of brown.

Today it's *fish*—not so much to eat
but to view through the glass plate

at the dentist's office—the color of fish
being mainly *orange* a color

it turns out
she likes a great deal.

Tomorrow it will be worries about fire—
is her hospital gown actually

fireproof (I will say it is, of course,
no harm in that) and she will be

relieved—she will listen to me and will
proudly walk through any fire.

Broken Hip

My mother in her high-tech
hospital bed hears music

I can't hear with the new
titanium screws holding her

Together *vibrating* and the ice pack
melts like Winter in the bag

On her hip. She's directing
the music—*I can almost see*

The music—the pages
of black notes like small precise

Obituaries flowing past like
a river of time from where

We were to where we are—
This music makes her smile

With her very own teeth
of which she's quite proud

And now the music seems
some inside joke some silly

Punch line summing up
this silly life—*I wish I could hear*

What she hears now—strings
rising up like simple heroism—

The single trumpet call like
morning coming on bright

As the empty tomb—and the voice—
her own voice—breaking—

Out of nowhere—
into this song—

Heavy

We go for a walk. She rides
in her chair. Four wheels.

Her Frankenstein Velcro shoes
rest on those foot rests.

She doesn't want to wear
the floppy straw hat from Italy

so she holds it tightly in her lap.
I'm looking down at the top

of her head. A new perspective.
Her white hair is not white—

it is transparent—absent of color.
The backs of her hands are bruised.

IVs from the hospital. Now we get
to a little park with the fake

Venetian canals. A model sailboat
remotely controlled by that fat guy

tilts in a puff of wind. I consider
running her chair down the ramp

into the water. There was a time
she would have enjoyed that.

But now her head has become
so heavy—too heavy to talk

Or watch the father and son
in the paddleboat. Too heavy for

anything. But this fall. A quick sleep.
A small nap. Her chin dropping down.

Yes

She hardly speaks except
to say "Yes"

Which she says often
as a general comment

A general attitude
of *Yes*

She lives in the moment
of *Yes*

An agreeable place
open as a lake

Open to the sky
with the trees along the edge

Floating in the substance
of *Yes*

This after much suffering
collapses of body and mind

A keening grief
she seems now to have forgotten

Because she's saying
Yes

To everyone and everything
that comes along

When all else fails
it is *Yes* that works

With its trailing open
"*es*"

And then a breath
before another breath

She

She doesn't know what
to do   She says

"I don't know what to do"
She can't eat or drink

She can't travel in a boat
down the Danube

She can breathe
pull at her sheets

She can pause in her breath
and look up

She—is being zeroed
in on   She

is now the target
the center in her own sights

The world and all of us
we rush away

And she—she's holding
as tightly as she can

Comfortable

She couldn't get comfortable
as if getting comfortable

Had become her job.
The process was slow. Such work

Getting comfortable. Her feet
were not getting cold. They said

Her feet were supposed to get cold.
She turned toward the wall.

Tried to pull at her nightgown.
Then turned back toward me. She

Seemed to think I could do something.
To make her comfortable. I wanted to.

So I held her. Leaning down toward
her bed from that straight-back chair.

My face—in the warm corner of her neck.
Her face at my neck too. Both our faces.

Awkward dancers. She was comfortable
that way—for a short time.

My Dead

They grow in number all the time
The cat, the Mother, the Father,
The grandparents, aunts, and uncles

Those I knew well and hardly at all
My best friend from when I was ten
The guy who sat with me in the back

Of the class where the tall kids lived
Bill the Shoemaker from Lyndale Avenue
The Irish poet with rounded handwriting

They live in *The Land of Echo, The Land
Of Reverb,* and I hear them between
The notes of the birds, the *plash* of the wave

On the smooth rocks. They show up
When I think of them, as if they always
Are waiting for me to remember

I drive by their empty houses
I put on their old sweaters and caps
I wear their wristwatches and spend

Their money. So now I'm in six places
At once—if not eighteen or twenty—
So many places to be thinking of them

Strange how quiet they are with their presence
So humble in the low song they sing
Not expecting that anyone will listen

The Blue Light

I asked her to come to me
in whatever way she chose

As the wind, as the ruffling
water, as the red maple leaf

So today I closed my eyes
halfway toward sleep

And she came in a blue light
blue as a tropical ocean

Turning toward a darker blue
as the Sun passed

Coming in blue waves coming
in from the side of my eyes

Somehow bathing me in blue—
a blue that seemed to be

Her gaze—turned to blue—
just as she was a few weeks ago

Her blue eyes and mine meeting
in that long long look—

Yesterday

As something like grief accumulated
I became squirrel-like
stowing it away for later.

Then I surprised myself on the way home
talking to my sister Kathleen
when I told her I loved her and how

Great she was with Mom how much
she had done for Mom.
And I caught myself my voice caught up

With myself and all the long grief or
something like long grief came up in me
in just a moment.

And I was a wreck (I am a wreck).
You could tell me any story about
a boy and a dog, if either dies

I will fall apart. And the grief
if that's what it is comes like Spring
rain on the roof of the car

Or tears or anything falling everything
falling so alive and breathing
toward the center of our Earth.

This is the dream we carry through the world that something fantastic will happen.

—Olav H. Hauge

Gettysburg

Remember how we got out of the car
at 1:30 a.m. in the foggy heat and passed
along the sidewalks through the seminary
campus and out to the field?
That field where Pickett made his charge.
And do you remember how
it was a time of ghosts everywhere
rising with the hot dew? And you
were a little boy and I was much
younger than I am now—*leaner*—
and we walked a ways into the field
the crickets and hoppers jumping up
before our feet and we didn't talk
at all all the way across the field
and when we went far enough a certain
distance I said something and you
agreed and so we turned back.

Ice House

We tried to read
our law books
in the dark ice house

While the little stove
burned hot
and condensation dripped

On the pages—
we also drank
a whole bottle

Of *Laphroaig*
single malt Scotch
and ate pistachios

And we didn't catch
any fish
until the very last

Moment late Sunday
when we hauled in
five good-sized walleyes

Threw them out
the door where they froze
fast in the deep snow

Twenty-five years
ago—I still remember
the blue ice hole

The light of the world
rising from the lake bed
blue sky in the water

A Vision

We drove a long time
around the endless city

Then—just as the twelve lanes
went down to six—

Going one way—I could
see Hell—*here*

It is—everyone rushing to get ahead
to nowhere—everyone late

For their appointments
with no one—everyone dying

As they run in place—the fuel
burning fast in the hot cylinders

The familiar exhaust like the sweat
of a dead father—the sad scrub

Brush on the edges of the road
like the pubic hair of an old mother

The disappointment in our
American way—which is this much

Con job—this much blow job—half
a dozen for less than half of that—

The weariness of early Spring—
the *so what* of the seed

The pushing ahead to somehow
push beyond—the chugging self—

The self-satisfaction—the false certainty—
the assurance of the liar—

The confidence of the confidence
man—all this and more—

The always more—the bumbling
Dagwood—the stupid neighbor—

The man with the gun—he always
shows up from the wings

The crazy man with the gun
who always shows up

The perfect timing of failure—
the tenderness of failure—

How we know at any moment
we could completely fail—fail

In a huge way—and then—
and then—we're gone from the party

We're gone—we're gone—we've
left already—Tell me—where's the meadow

Where she walked? Where's the shore
where he paused to think?

This special American
sadness—this pretend—this elixir—

This shoe polish—this dye in the hair—
this pretend America—*but still*—

The little family still—The Madonna—
The Child—the lovely stupid

Joseph—the meal at the table—the moment
of the meal—the moment of the breath—

Turns out—we are in Indiana—
we have always been in Indiana

In this close hollow by the river—
The trees—*the Sun in the trees*—

The Sun in the trees in the hills—
you can tell it's the river—

It's always been the river—
taking everything away—

Children of Myanmar Who Behave
Like Japanese Soldiers

Most of the children described
being shot or blown up in their former lives.

Two said they'd been burned alive
and one said he had his throat cut

at the zoo in Rangoon. You can question
their memories. They were all born

after 1945 when there were no Japanese
soldiers alive in Burma, no Japanese soldiers

anywhere. The report details the distance
from where the Japanese soldiers died

to where the Burmese children were born,
in meters, sometimes 30, sometimes 800.

All that dying of Japanese soldiers in Burma.
Burmese children born in the aftermath.

The children exhibited behaviors that were
Japanese-like—nostalgia for Japan,

a preference for raw fish, strong tea,
wearing trousers, belts, and boots.

When the Burmese children saw planes overhead,
they yearned for Japan, their home in a different life.

I don't expect you to believe any of this,
but there is a report with impressive graphs and charts.

Wood Smoke

In Springtime among the songs
of the birds the smell

of a fire in the distance
the long memory of smoke

smoke on the skin
huddled knees

Our bodies we don't even
realize how odd it is

that we fuck and shit and pee
and move on

and eat birds and leaves
and walk upright and *sleep*

and wake to smell smoke
from burning wood

Windows On The World

After Ellis Island we went up
to *Windows On The World*
to have a drink and look out
at the world. Rich asked for
"the drink Cary Grant drank
in *North By Northwest*," and
the cocktail waitress without a pause
without any hint of uncertainty
said "That would be a *Gibson*."
So Rich had several *Gibsons*
left a huge tip. He would never know
how the world would turn.

Museum

If you walk through Ancient
Greek and Roman Statuary

You will come to the Code
of Hammurabi. If you go too far

You will arrive at the Northern
Painters of the Low Countries.

You will not be able to exit
that gallery until you deal

With French Decorative Arts—
tables, chairs, little bowls—

All in gold, somehow so sad
and *kitschy*. You will know

You have inadvertently entered
the next building if you find

Yourself in Dada beside the Dali
Exhibit. Turn back to the left

Toward the Egyptian tombs or
sarcophagi—the human mummies

Are elsewhere, but you can see
the cat mummies in the far right corner.

Lacemaking is on the Fifth Floor,
but Paintings of Lacemakers are on Seven.

Overwhelming Landscapes are hung
near every ceiling. Just look up.

Monumental Battle Scenes
are all out on loan, except for those

Involving Napoleon. Napoleon shows up
at least once—on every floor.

Copley Square Hotel

I walked by that place today
in the rushed snow in a Boston

version of *Dr. Zhivago*—the wet
snow sticking to my sport coat—

Entirely cold—and you might be
Lara—somewhere far away.

I see now it was never
an elegant hotel but they did

put us up in a suite of rooms
and charged us for a single

because we were young and fresh
and just married. The whole world

came down to that abundant bed,
the bowed windows looking out

on the street. The lamps
lit your face in a nineteenth

century light. Sometimes we can
slip behind the curtain—come out

someplace else—where it may be
summer—where it was summer

and there was music
rising up from the square.

Devotions

I saw this after Mass at the Church
of San Felipe Neri, San Miguel de Allende,

An ancient Indian woman walking
backwards down the marble aisle

Keeping her eyes on the Eucharist, walking
backwards, as she has done since she

Was a little girl, her face now coppery,
wrinkled, but her eyes lively, brown,

Fixed on the altar, walking backwards,
carefully, past the sculpted effigy

Of San Felipe Neri, lying in his final bed,
dressed in gold vestments, and the woman

I have named Maria, continues to walk
backwards, deliberately, but without

Hesitation, she is so certain she will not
fall, or if she falls, she will recover

And her devotions somehow fill
the Church of San Felipe Neri, as others

Quickly leave to go back to their lives,
while she practices her habit of walking

Backwards, until she reaches the great
oak door, and only then does she

Turn to walk into the new Sun, new
every day for her, the streets again

Rise up, and she has taken and given
all of her attention, she has given

Everything to reach this moment
of walking forward, more slowly now,

Because while she attended her devotions
she was light, as light as that bird—

Yellow and green, flying in circles
above her

Café

After walking a long way
you need to stop.

This is a good place because
there are straw chairs

A little table, a tiny cup
of strong coffee, and your breath

Which is even and low.
You notice the others who pause.

They are in the same state of *Pause,*
while the old couple passing by—

The man in a yellow cashmere
sportcoat and his wife

In the gray sweater—appear
like songbirds back from Africa.

There should be a fountain.
You hear a fountain in the background.

You seem to have caught up
to yourself somehow—in this *Pause.*

The Sun. The clouds above
that mansard roof.

How is it? That every moment
led to this precise one?

Cathedral

This is the seat of your dreams
and the range of your imagination.

It operates as a case within
which you aspire. Its towers

Are irregularly shaped—one contains
the bells—the other silence.

You enter through a small wooden
door in the far corner.

When you are inside, you realize
the air of God is cold.

The light through stained-glass
is the passing idea you could live forever.

The mouse scraping its nails
on the lead organ pipes

Is every pet you've ever loved.
Being inside—you still can sense

The town square is out there—
the cousins, the grandchildren—

The horses and the horse shit.
You are compelled to wait here—*inside.*

The altar boy swings the censer
against its chain while the little

Sandalwood cube burns low
and the smoke flares up and out.

Remember all those nights around
the fire when you wanted

A vaulted roof above you—
to be inside?

A roof decorated with golden stars
each painted by hand in the dark.

Cemetery

I must be odd. How I love
these small cities—the vanity

of the dead with their quaint
marble houses. Their stark names

etched in gold. The way the place
gives itself over to the place

of nature where the privileged
citizens are squirrels and birds.

Where is the simple longing
for restaurants, dry cleaners,

hardware stores? No banks
necessary, no cafés. No need

for a car. No need for shoes or
those who repair shoes. No need

for feet or fingers. Nonetheless
what happiness in this city—more

than enough time between breaths—
everything worn down to the bone.

Red Wing Correctional Facility

Along the bluffs, the limestone Main Building
has the manner of 19th century discipline
and retribution for somewhat small juvenile
wrongs. The wrongs are greater now, I'm thinking,
as I get buzzed in, escorted through several doors,
and taken in an unmarked car about half a block
to the room of boys, black boys, laughing and strutting,
and I'm there to talk about poetry and life, so I start
with Walt Whitman, to blow out the pipes because
you want to blow the dust out of that old church music
to find one's own song and Walt is the best, and the boys
are listening, each of them listening, from Chicago
and New Orleans and Minneapolis, listening as I read
"Crossing Brooklyn Ferry" and they are right there with Walt
right there with his voice which they already know somehow
and I suggest what poetry can do, that it can cross mountains,
escape prisons (they laugh like *yeah sure*), that words
can go to the stars and back, and by breathing Shakespeare's sonnet
you can inhabit Shakespeare's very vocal chords. So,
we're going along like this and I mention *The Soul*, not in some
religious sense but in the sense that each of us has a *Soul*, that sense
we get in a moment that there is something magnificent in us
that is not us but somehow is and the boys are listening very
closely to my words from each of their places around the table—
Omar, Ken, Josh, Jordan, James—and I get them in the mood
to write and they start writing, some in small precise script,
some in blocky letters, some in flourishes that end
with a celebrity signature and now I have them read
their favorite poem of the poems they've just written and now
they read their second-favorite poem until they've read everything
they've written today and I say *Big voices, men, let's have these
big slow voices* and they get courage in their words each one
of the words they picked and I ask them to write a poem called
Red Wing and they moan a poem called *Red Wing* which is

the *facility* within which they are to be *corrected* and I have them
begin with *The River*, then *The Trees*, then *The Stars*
and they say unremarkable things about the river and the trees,
and the stars they never see because it's always too late for stars
or too early and the lights, the lights are always too bright.

Leaving

If I were beside
a Chinese river in the 6th century
I would pick few words.

Someone is going away
down the path
that someone may turn.

Because we are 6th century
Chinese friends
we are sad to take leave.

We have pet crickets
at home in elegant
little enameled boxes.

If you can pay attention
to a pet cricket
leave-taking must be hard.

When we next meet
it will be Winter
the snow on the mountain.

The fast fire
in the black stove.
Can you believe

We are atop
this Jade Mountain again
the cold river rushing through?

Song

At the funeral for the young man
I'm trying to sing
the complicated song

And I'm running out of
breath
there are too many

Changes in direction
in this song—
some parts

Are just for the choir
they sound great
up above in their loft

Then the men sing
and that's surprising—
the women

Are tentative
when they sing
but sweet

The song is mostly about Jesus
who I think would be
a little embarrassed

With all the attention
at the same time
he might like the sound

We sound like birds
on a long summer day—
the good young man

Remains dead—we know that—
but still we want
to make a song

Because it seems it could last
forever or just long enough
to get us through

The Flow

Of people from the L Line underground
headed for the A, C, E trains—I can tell
I'm getting old but still have this desire

to move through across up and down toward
my next future which might just be
dinner somewhere or an appointment

that compels me—everyone else has the same
deep wisdom about getting home or to dinner
or to the girl on the bed five flights up—

someone said: *New York City is the greatest
experiment in democracy*—and—*If it doesn't
work here it won't work anywhere*

Right now—in this vestibule of the subway—
the stairs up and down—the signs and arrows—
this *forum*—which we pass over across and

through—appears to be the landscape
of every dream we've ever had or will—
this dream of getting through—it feels like

a full-court press of the fortunate living—
we all seem to glow from a single light
that is somehow both within and without—

Talking

They will figure out someday
that we've been talking

To one another all the time—
talking in our dreams—sending

Pictures to one another of Paradise—
sending love and prayers—

Sending our best wishes—talking
non-stop with the living and the dead—

Back and forth there being
no real difference between the living

And the dead and it is our destiny
to talk in banter like Pat and Mike

Or Petruchio and Kate or Norman Mailer
and Gore Vidal—talking all the time

About everything we see and think
and feel—and even though

We imagine we are alone—it seems
sometimes like desert isolation—

We are talking to ourselves or
another version of ourselves or

The actual *you*—or our version of you—
talking to Abraham Lincoln or Emily

Dickinson—and they talk back—at first
in a whisper and then the full deal—

talking—talking out loud—this
endless talking—we can't get enough—

Edgar Mitchell Coming Home

Halfway home from the Moon
Edgar Mitchell Astronaut No. 27
sixth man to walk on the Moon
was overwhelmed with the sense
that the restraints and boundaries
of his flesh and bones had fallen away
and that the molecules of his body
had once been manufactured
in the furnace of an ancient
generation of stars and Al and Stu
beside him in the rolling command
module were made of the same
stardust—whatever was happening
to Edgar Mitchell was intensely
poignant and personal—
this sense
that he took in the whole cosmos

Treasure

I've always thought there was an island
where in the sand forty paces here

fifty paces toward the tallest palm tree
there would be the chest and the treasure.

Now I think if you climb up to the top
of the tree I sit under

and look down there will be a chest
within which there's a heart

still beating regularly still unclogged
within which there is

a mirror or the blue sky
reflective. And *X* will mark the spot.

The Field

Remember that meadow up above the ridge
where the dog ran around in circles
and we were tired from the climb up
and everything was tilted sideways
including the running in circles
of the ecstatic dog his bright tongue
lapping at the air and we were
leaning into the heart of the field
where no battle ever took place
where no farmer ever bothered
to turn the soil yet everything
seemed to have happened there everything
seemed to be happening at once enough
so we've never forgotten how full the field
was and how we were there too and full

Acknowledgments

My thanks to the editors of the following magazines where some of these poems first appeared:

American Life in Poetry: "My Dead."
The Forward Book of Poetry: "Red Wing Correctional Facility." Finalist for the Forward Prize in Poetry.
Great River Review: "The Basement," "Copley Square Hotel," and "Broken Hip."
Hennepin County Lawyer: "Resume."
Legal Studies Forum: "Self-Portrait as a Busy Person," "Self-Portrait as a Patch of Dirt," and "Self-Portrait as a Dog,"
Lief Magazine: "Yesterday," "In the sunlight," "Treasure," "Wind in Spring," "12 Years Old," "Roasted Chicken," and "Gettysburg."
Mudfish: "Stray Words" and "Heavy."
The New Republic: "Catwork" and "My Dead."
Ploughshares: "Song."
Poetry City USA, Vol. 2: "Leaving."
Thirty Two: "Our Midwestern Sky."
Troubadour International "Red Wing Correctional Facility." Third Place in Poetry Contest 2013
Water~Stone Review: "Yes."

Special thanks to The Anderson Center in Red Wing, in Minnesota, where many of these poems were written, and the Minnesota State Arts Board for an Artist's Initiative Grant which gave me the time to put this collection together.

Many thanks to all my friends in the poetry community in the Twin Cities, especially Joyce Sutphen, Connie Wanek, Louis Jenkins, Garrison Keillor, Eric Utne, Jeri Reilly, Patricia Kirkpatrick, Robert Hedin, Freya Manfred, Alison McGhee, Jim Rogers, Michael Moos, Becca Barniskis, Todd Boss, Sharon Chmielarz, Kirsten Dierking, Liz Weir, who read these poems and have been very supportive along the way.

Thanks to Al Davis, Thom Tammaro, and everyone at New Rivers Press for providing me with a home for my work. Thanks especially to Nayt Rundquist, Mikaila Norman, Desiree Miller, and Jin Thieschafer for their great work on this book.

Finally, thanks, thanks, thanks, thanks Kate, Elizabeth, Maeve, and Frank—you dear ones!

About the Author

Tim Nolan received a BA in English from the University of Minnesota, an MFA from Columbia University, and a JD from William Mitchell College of Law. He is an attorney in Minneapolis.

During his time at Columbia, Nolan was the managing editor of *Columbia: A Magazine of Poetry & Prose*, and for five years he was the primary poetry reader at *The Paris Review*. He has been writing and publishing poems for more than forty years. His work has appeared in *The Gettysburg Review*, *The Nation*, *The New Republic*, *Ploughshares*, and many other publications.

In 2014, his poem "Red Wing Correctional Facility" was a finalist for the Forward Poetry Prize in London. He has received grants from the Minnesota State Arts Board, a residency at the Anderson Center, and was recently a finalist for the *Mudfish Poetry Prize* judged by Edward Hirsch.

This is Nolan's third book with New Rivers Press. *The Sound of It*, appeared in 2008 and was a finalist for the Minnesota Book Awards, and *And Then* appeared in 2012.

About New Rivers Press

New Rivers Press emerged from a drafty Massachusetts barn in winter 1968. Intent on publishing work by new and emerging poets, founder C. W. "Bill" Truesdale labored for weeks over an old Chandler & Price letterpress to publish three hundred fifty copies of Margaret Randall's collection, *So Many Rooms Has a House But One Roof.*

Nearly four hundred titles later, New Rivers, a non-profit and now teaching press based since 2001 at Minnesota State University Moorhead, has remained true to Bill's goal of publishing the best new literature—poetry and prose—from new, emerging, and established writers.

New Rivers Press authors range in age from twenty to eighty-nine. They include a silversmith, a carpenter, a geneticist, a monk, a tree-trimmer, and a rock musician. They hail from cities such as Christchurch, Honolulu, New Orleans, New York City, Northfield (Minnesota), and Prague.

Charles Baxter, one of the first authors with New Rivers, calls the press "the hidden backbone of the American literary tradition." Continuing this tradition, in 1981 New Rivers began to sponsor the Minnesota Voices Project (now called Many Voices Project) competition. It is one of the oldest literary competitions in the United States, bringing recognition and attention to emerging writers. Other New Rivers publications include the American Fiction Series, the American Poetry Series, New Rivers Abroad, and the Electronic Book Series.

Please visit our website **newriverspress.com** for more information.